ACUITY

KENDALL DONAR

AN IMPRINT OF P.L.A.N.E PUBLISHING

ACUITY

Copyright © 2016 Kendall Donar

All rights reserved.

Printed in the United States of America. No part of this book may be used or reproduced in any manner whatsoever without written permission except in the case of brief quotations embodied in critical articles and reviews. For information address P.L.A.N.E Publishing Co. 8380 Country Walk Dr. Unit C, Pensacola, FL 32514.

P.L.A.N.E Publishing books may be purchased for educational, business, or sales promotional use. For information please write: P.L.A.N.E Publishing Co. 8380 Country Walk Dr. Unit C, Pensacola, FL 32514.

ACKNOWLEDGMENTS

These poems, written between 2011 and 2016 are a part of an archive of pieces which were assembled by Kendall Donar during various stages of growth, introspection and reflection throughout that time.

Front & back coverphotograph designed by Kendall Donar, Danielle Buffong and Frantz Pierre.

ISBN-10:0692661859

ISBN-13: 978-0692661857

FOR RONALD & LINDA DONAR

4

TABLE OF CONTENTS

ACUITY

Star Gazing

Dear little woman nestled and resting in the reassuring lap of true love,

Hello.

I don't even know your name but the Universe has taught me that inevitably, you will grow.

So as you grow, I beseech you.

Tiny, promising pulse of light shining bright off in the not so distant corner of my sight;

Take this wisdom with you as you go.

#1

Be mindful of your mind.

It is a jewel far too bright to stay buried in the dark caverns of society's dark mines.

Let it guide you.

And when the time arises to rise up and accept your kingdom,

Confine yourself in a tower of truth.

Crown yourself with contentment.

Effervesce excellence and allow your King to find you.

#2

If you ever have to glance behind you,

Do so with forgiveness and acceptance.

We were created for giving and for getting love beloved.

Only the foolish choose to neglect this.

#3

There is no making up for perfection.

Every atom in your face was birthed from stardust.

And before even a single piece of you was selected

to be placed in its present section,

The Universe held and election.

Every decision was unanimous.

Your beauty is magnanimous.

So guard your heart from humanity's self-hate based perception.

#4

The Universe is a circle; so be open.

Having real things lodged down on the inside of you

is the truest definition of choking.

#5

Breathe and live.

Live and breathe.

In every drop there is an ocean.

In every sequoia tree, a seed.

#6

Be free and be you.

Never apologize for the color of your iris.

Within it springs forth a promise so deep

that it would make your ancestors day dream of Olympic style high
diving.

Into you, there are treasures buried the world has yet even to dream.

#7

The sun will rise tomorrow no matter how dark it may seem.

#8

Keep company with wisdom,

invite knowledge out for coffee

and regularly converse with understanding.

#9

Ground yourself in your truth and you'll seldom need to ever question the validity of your standing.

#10

Jump.

Higher than you can see

and farther than you believe.

Without the chance of failure there would be no chance to succeed.

#11

Take heed

to all the lessons that this life will teach you.

All the roads you will travel and passersby who will greet you.

For a star as bright as you was never meant to burn silent.

Radiation too intense.

Love shade far too ultra in violet.

#12

They will attempt to make you quite.

Throw flares at your soul.

When they do, be cool

and from your core, sling forth gold.

#13

Enjoy the journey and appreciate your way.

The river flows forward and this is the whole truth of the way.

So until we meet again, I wish you peace, light and your full number of days.

Sincerely,

A lowly passerby, simply star struck by your rays.

I AM FROM

I AM FROM a stone's throw from the beach

but very little sand ever having been beneath my feet.

I AM FROM the old Nickelodeon simple and plain.

Teenage Mutant Ninja Turtles, Power Rangers and such of the same.

I AM FROM a strong sense of self-worth.

Instilled in me by a Mother who made it a point to point out to me

those bright, white points in the sky

at a point when I

was unsure of my why

and remind I

that the very hands that composed their beauty and majesty

are the selfsame hands that lavishly

handed me to her.

I AM FROM Sunday school on Sunday mornings.

Sitting anxiously waiting for Sunday stories

spoke in the vernacular tongue of rhythm, blues, and rhetorical pourings

that pour forth from the pit that pulls at heart strings

and cries out to lost souls

and old church ladies who would tell us

that if we came and patiently paid the Lord his due on Sunday

then they would give us a dollar to buy a sundae

at the Dairy Queen across the street

which sat on the hill

to which we looked for our strength.

I AM FROM can't miss Saturday magic & puppet shows at the mall.

With a handful of popcorn in hand

and a Clifford the Big Red Dog shade stain

on my white Clifford the Big Red Dog shirt.

I AM FROM summertime strolls with my cousins through the projects in route to the Jullop Lady's house.

Armed with 3 quarters,

innocence and a dream of quenched fatigue

that came like clockwork

after an hour's work

of mowing and raking the yard of my Grandmother's castle.

Which was nestled in the heart of a ghetto darkness that never seemed to be quite strong enough to breach her stately walls.

I AM FROM being looked after and brought up by a collection of community and family even when I was unaware.

I AM FROM hip-hop, blues, r&b, pop, jazz, rock, gospel, and techno because that was all we had.

I AM FROM laughing until I cry, trying until I fly, and forgiving until one more time after forever.

I AM FROM a legacy of leaving a legacy and I carry a piece of home with me wherever I go.

I AM FROM ME

Nothing in the Highest

My religion is nothing

Nothing watches over me

Nothing orders my steps

Nothing died for my sins

Nothing paid my debts

Nothing gave me a new life

Nothing made me brand new

Nothing knows my heart

Nothing is my peace

Nothing is my savior

Nothing made me in its image

Nothing is my anchor

Nothing is omnipresent

Nothing is omniscient

Nothing created the trees

the yeast

the seas

and all the beautiful fishes

Nothing showed me mercy

Nothing showed me grace

Nothing saved me from my enemies

Nothing gave me strength

Nothing began a great work in me

Nothing surely will finish it

Nothing knew my pain

Nothing came to diminish it

Nothing never lied to me

Nothing loves me more than I will ever know

Nothing never left my side

Nothing sanctifies my soul

Nothing is the way

the truth

and life

Without which there would be

Resin Dew

Leave everything better than you found it, every time.

Including people.

Take away a lesson from everything you find, every time.

Including life.

Love will always leave a mark and take a piece.

Thank you for the math lesson.

It can never be packed into word boxes.

Doesn't work that way.

Take your time.

Make the time.

Share your time, every time.

It is the present.

It can only be presented.

Thank you for showing me your love.

It was all ways beautiful.

It was all ways amazing.

All ways smiling.

Laughing.

Long, long suffering.

Bear chested and vulnerable.

Unashamed and breakable.

Unafraid and frightening in compassion.

Gentle as lioness caress to cub.

Shape of love,

dinner table blushed brown memories.

Thank you for the end pieces first,

every time.

Best hugs I've ever known.

Sweetest soul we've ever been loaned.

Glad you're home.

O ye gates turned fences link chained.

Difficult to rejoice in the morning through the mourning and pain.

The Ancestors say,

dew is necessary

and natural

and expected.

Your gift has filled us full.

In due time, every time.

Missing you already,

loving you still,

every time.

The persistence of pReS(c)ents(se)

I wish I would have frozen your face in liquid nitrogen.

Should have written a computer program in JavaScript

to display the way that you would jettisoned my quilt into the orbit of the gentle gas giants.

Let it levitate resolute as a rain suspended in cumulonimbus clouds over a somber Seattle Saturday

and then

crash it back down into my world.

With all the fiery poise of an ancient igneous astronaut

destined to make contact

with the bipedal, tongue split monsters which once populated the Yucatan.

But then,

stop

and gently caress the soil of my soul

and make life brood over the waters of my skin;

Genesis 1.

I wish I would have captured the taste of your voice calling my name in my gut back then.

Because it was so guttural.

So loveable.

So able to love.

I wish I was able;

totally and completely,

to hug the very basement roots of your life tree.

I wish for the shade of your kinky satin

to again contract and constrict my myostatin,

rescue me from these porch swing yellow jackets

and encircle my spirit with the hex that only a converted demon could create.

I wish it wasn't too late.

I wish we had more time.

But in my quiet place,

I know we do.

Peace With Ends

Fortune cookie say,

peace comes from within.

Seek it from yourself.

Fortune cookie say,

do you find difficulty in opportunities

or opportunity in difficulties?

Fortune cookie say,

education is the movement of soul from darkness to light.

Fortune cookie say,

peace is the key to joy.

Fortune cookie say.

Fortune cookie say.

Fortune cookies says.

Fortune cookies contain great fortunes within empty pockets.

Ahab's Compass

The man sat there for years.

Never missed an appointment.

He was a patient.

He waited,

patiently.

Waited for some bus

going someplace

at sometime

driven by nobody

expected by no one.

In the middle of the sunrise.

Serrated, separated and beautiful.

He grew to depend on their scraps.

Ask and you shall receive.

Never leave

and you might find yourself.

Amassed together under the seesaw shade of stingy willow trees, the man found nirvana looking into a two way mirror at nighttime in misty moonlight.

Writing a love letter, in love language with crimson pen strokes on the back of a receipt.

Hiding under the bed from the monsters of men who mob in silence on the corners of darkness; plotting their escape.

Crawling on its hands and knees across fields of broken, brown glass and pungent purple lilies; in slow motion.

He found it open.

Door screen serrated, separated, beautiful and waving in the void.

He found Namaste on the good side of a cracked doorway.

So he waited.

Until the coast were cleared.

Bare Aums

I am afraid to set my triceps ablaze.

Out of the fear that one day in May

after the April rain has gone away

and the flowers of May have been delayed

by one day too late,

I may resort to solitary self-immolation.

You see,

there exist these certain times to me

when this life that I lead seems to be

Hell bent on bending every ounce of Heaven out of me.

Macerating its intestines in hand blenders and handing the blend to me.

Saying, see.

The true hue of black boy broken dreams is blue.

And you are no exception to the rule.

There is nothing more pitiable than a willfully captured, castrated and broken bull.

Shit, this plate through which you have staked great pains to create looks great but

1000 and 1 apologies to you.

I apologize but I am full

and I am tired

and I no longer wish to dine on lies.

I wonder.

Do flies make wish to dine on lives?

Is it pleasurable for them?

Do they perceive the irony of the situation as a witness that is inherently bare?

Like the fact that, it is a fact of life that the little things eat away at you only when you cease to care.

Yes.

There.

There I find myself inconsolably aware

of the steel etched countenance of the universe whisking back her hair

and cracking a smirk.

Not a smile.

Just enough space between sub dimensional membranes to say,

hey.

You should stay for a while.

It's nice here.

You might like it.

And so I do.

And I do,

for a while.

But just like those 90's era black barbers in Brooklyn,

rest assured that it too will inevitably begin to fade.

And on those days,

my perception of the grave sways

as it begins to look eerily like a much needed home away.

From Hell,

I have wished for well.

Then found myself fish food.

Prepared prey for whales.

Consumed by this heartless, darkness inside of all wells

there exist a tragically, magic dichotomy of taxonomy.

Whales

can swim through vast seas and oceans

because, not in spite of the fact that they are hollow.

Wells

Are not too full of their surroundings nor themselves.

Wells

can be sources of great doom if you fall in

but from the outside, great wealth.

Wells

tend to teach this truth very well.

Tiny things amassed over time tend to terrorize the mind

Hell

is a prison of poorly promulgated prisms.

Cells

divide and deride us to a point of self-isolation.

Within ourselves

there are shelves

upon shelves

upon shelves

stocked full of emptiness.

Or is it just me

To me,

sometimes this life seems to be

an old, decrepit, dirty, run down train station.

At the entrance to its gates, I sit patient;

weighting for my ticket.

Home they say is wherever you make it; so make it.

But at times I feel, I surely will not make it.

Here.

So I steer away from family, friends and piers.

Wooden splinters suspended over sure destruction pierce

me onto splintered trees and then wait for further instruction.

Peers.

Physical manifestations of cosmic juxtaposition.

Cheers.

They say death is just a reversed introduction.

Years of pain, regret and tac toed silhouettes

have conspired in rooms lit by shame's luminescence

to brew a preposterously potent batch of evanescent effervescence.

Crown bowed, hands united I pray and God blesses.

Resigned to reposition, I give invitation to its essence; clear.

Moving diaphragm, seas and mountain in order to get away.

In the heart of the mourning I've mapped out my escape.

Over here.

This way.

Now lay there,

totally and utterly prostrate.

Now wait.

As I begin to burn this goatly flesh.

Interweaving its form into a goatly mesh.

Yes, I have placed ash in my cloth and disaster in my breath.

I am the second son of David thrusting himself into the Koresh

in order for my ghost to find a piece of the rest.

I pledge, my specter shall spectate no more.

This door, remain resolute no more.

I lobby the congress of my Father's house to release its stores.

And give unto me a Mississippian type of EBT.

Card holding member of the lost tribe of give us, us free.

Dumb, I admit.

But when you get this sick

you swear you can see the truth lying in the face of an illusion.

Nothing needn't be proven.

Even losing can seem like the greatest gain of all.

On the day when in humanity gravity loses its hope

and makes the conscious decision to let go of the rope

remember;

the ground will be the first to fall.

Accouchement

Baby, it's gone be beautiful.

It's gone be a sight to see.

Now, it's gone be hard to breathe at first but I promise,

it's gone be all right little one

just you wait and see.

It's gone be mesmerizing.

It's gone be spellbinding and full of wizardry.

It's gone spew forth the fuel for the dragons fire

like a hot spring of death wine

and announce an altar call

for all the wizards within earshot to hear

and take heed.

Believe you me, you gone see.

It's gone be attractive.

It's gone be damn near radioactive.

It's gone burn hard and long

long after it's done burned out

but in the end, you gone see.

It's gone be relaxing.

Like the sound of yo' granny calling you inside

for a suppa comprised of

smothered pork chops,

buttermilk biscuits with molasses,

freshly squeezed lemonade with ice cubes in chilled glasses

and a nice sized slice of her homemade, Georgia peach, cream pie.

Or the screams of your ancestors bones

buried in the morse code mausoleums erect on the outside of your neck.

Baptizing and reminding you in cold sweat

to be inside before the street lights come on

and the ghost come out.

It's gone be no doubt

what this is about.

It's gone awake something in yo' cells.

Shhh.

Don't you hear it?

The flickering flames

and faint concert being played

of fleeing roach, grasshopper and nigger off in the distant southern night

wish to tell you a tale.

Listen well.

It's gone be one hell of a night.

It's gone be like,

if God left the backdoor to heaven unlocked

and cracked open out of spite;

on his way back from an evening

of fiery play in the playground of the devil's mistress.

Only to leave an inordinate amount of omniscient footprints

in the anguish and bloodshed which stain the broken clay roads of Hell.

From her doorsteps to his mansion.

Cuz God knows everythang.

And them demons know where they going.

All prodigal bastards return to Heaven.

This shall be the Crow of the law.

And if ya' ain't know befoe' then young'n you best get ta act'n like ya' know'n.

It's gone be snowing.

6, 7 to 11 inches of white privilege

suspended above the earth.

It's gone be white's only posters

written in black letters posted above a spoon silver water fountain

as you lay there dying of thirst.

It's gone be blood.

It's gone be heritage.

It's gone be brotherhood and love.

It's gone be enough tears falling from grace

to fill 10,000 made in Washington,

distilled in Mississippi moonshine mugs.

It's gone be a sponge

seated on the shoulders of every

God fearing, good Christian man and woman.

Ready to soak it in.

It's gone be sin.

But we gone have to do it.

It's gone be a 97 year old

blind niggra boy,

pants full of his own shit.

Wading through a 100 yard reservoir pond our own sewage.

It's gone be 12 feet high,

6 feet wide and drenched in lighter fluid.

It's gone be fluid.

It's gone be music.

It's gone swing.

It's gone sing a song of white light,

black flight,

rebel might,

and Good Ol' Dixie.

It's gone be Dixie.

It's gone be home.

Acuity

When I was young,

My Father told me to write legibly.

He told me it was an important skill to learn

in order to prepare me for the inevitable twist and turns

which he discerned

lay in wait right ahead of me.

He told me to consciously make my thoughts clear

and my words aesthetically pleasing.

He told me to always press the pen to the page with pure purpose

and a refined sense of reason.

He told me.

Son, in your writing be as easily divisible as the seasons.

Clearly present in your absence

so they will never be asking

from whence you go

nor when you will be leaving.

He told me.

Son, it is okay to be misleading,

but never lie with your lead.

See, your pencil is a most powerful member of your body;

with a mind of its own.

So please, be mindful of where you place your head.

He told me.

Son, be safe.

He told me.

Son, never be safe.

He told me.

Son, always write with the confidence of knowledge that stems from
knowing this.

That if ever in this game of life you are thrown out while trying to steal 3rd,

you can always run right back to home plate.

For a home plate.

Free of charge.

He told me.

Son, be safe when you need to and not when you don't.

He told me.

Son, it is the hands that pull the oars but it is the oars which pull the boat.

He told me.

Son, make your writing a soap and use it to clean yourself of this filth filled existence.

He told me.

Son, find your place, take your seat and sign your name into existence.

Force them to listen.

Be insistent.

Persistent.

Even if it pisses them off.

He told me.

Son, be alone at times and wait for your soul to write you.

Let it incite you

and then, write back;

legibly.

He told me.

Son, write for those for whom it was intended

and for those who might one day read it.

He told me.

Son, you know, you write real, real good

but it don't matter if can't nobody read it.

He told me.

Son, slow down.

Don't write so fast.

Please, take your time.

He told me.

Son, a man should always stand like a man

and his words should always start on the line.

He told me.

Sometimes;

Son, it's not what you say, it's how it looks.

He told me.

Always;

Son, it's not what you write, it's how it crooks.

He told me.

Son, you are brilliant.

You should really start working on that book.

I told him.

Father, I hear you, but it's not as easy as it looks.

He told me.

Son, it doesn't matter how it looks.

Just make sure I can read it.

Intelligent Black Man the Super Man

Whoosh!

What is that walking past that tree?

Is it a hood, is it a thug, or maybe a thief?

It's 8 hours too black to be walking these streets.

Is it a feign, murderer, drug dealer or maybe all three?

All bigots take aim steady, your colorful quips!

Make sure to whisper, quiet your lips.

All women with purses tighten your grips!

Increase your stride, God speed to your hips!

All children in range take heed and head home.

Parents, place your finger over the nine on your phone.

All drivers move swiftly to lock your doors.

Protect any possession that you wish to keep yours.

Oh no, your worst fears were correct it seems!

Intelligent Black Man the Super Man!

That's me.

Civilians cannot comprehend the power that I possess.

To strike fear in their hearts and cause them much stress.

Maybe it is my music, my hair, or my dress.

Or maybe it is the quantum physics book that I clinch to my chest.

Or maybe it is my swag, the confidence of my walk.

Or maybe it is my vernacular, the grace of my talk.

Or maybe it is the beauty of the skin that I am in that causes you to judge without knowing what is within.

Whatever the case, I refuse to let them block me.

No kryptonite in sight, only I can stop me.

For I know, in the end I can only be me.

Intelligent Black Man, the Original Super Man!

Yes, that is me.

mYneRbrAynetRimMehrsahNthEma dDerOvmipurSupsHionUvmisUlphrE ephleksion

Who am I?

Ultimately, I don't know yet.

I will never know.

That's the beauty to me.

I get to find out.

That's what this life is.

Or is it that ultimately, I am everything.

I have no end.

I am an equation with no solution.

An algorithm for eternity.

I am universe in microcosm.

I can be many things.

I am that which I choose to be.

Labels?

I am male, human, black, African American, earthling, North American, American, straight, strange, afraid of a lot, Son of Ron and Linda, Brother of Keenan and Toya (and others), cousin, grandson, nephew, uncle, liar, honest, confused, self-aware, pretentious, forgetful, sincere, friendly, deserting, distant, afraid, student, graduate, initiate, enlightened, Team Android, angry looking, kind hearted, soft spoken, loud, funny, serious, meek, selfish, vain, writer, listener, speaker, smeller of magnolia petals, different, ashamed, proud, respectful, respectable, sensual, sexual, prudish, well meaning, complicated, undone, complete, work in progressive motion towards construction with casual stops along the way to take in the view, amazed, afraid, driven, timid, ambitious, fearful, forgetful, wise, knowledgeable, understanding, ignorant, plain, special, artsy, long winded, a lot, a little, a little bit in between, outside, inside, outcast, introspective, cruel, dreamer, pessimist, optimist, realist, sophist, crazy, cool, insane, sane, afraid, more or less becoming brave.

Who am I?

I don't know yet...we'll see.

Here Lies the Little Boy

Here lies the little boy.

In his bed, but no longer asleep.

Here lies the little boy.

This secret he forever will keep.

Here lies the little boy.

His innocence replaced with shame.

Here lies the little boy.

Too young to make sense of such pain.

Here lies the little boy.

His tears were too afraid scream.

Here lies the little boy.

Robbed blind of his vision and dreams.

Here lies the little boy.

A happy little boy he once was.

Here lies the little boy.

Face down in a puddle blood.

Here lies the little boy.

Immobile and just barely breathing.

Here lies the little boy.

Real monsters don't wear mask in the evening.

Here lies the little boy.

Beheaded and shredded to pieces.

Here lies the little boy.

For his soul, the Lord now reaches.

Here lies the little boy.

In the place where no one can see.

Here lies the little boy.

I've buried him here, inside of me.

And To You

There was nothing else to do.

What else was I supposed to do?

I mean really, what else could I possibly do?

At the mention of such news,

where was I to go?

Tell me where do shell robbed baby turtles turn to hide

when skies fall like shattered wino glasses

and stone cold cosmonauts collide into their skin?

It was 2 hours, 22 minutes and amen in the morning when I last looked
at the computer clock.

Before I managed to lay my eyes to rest for a while.

Less than an hour later

you left cage

and then laid yours to rest for ever and a while.

I'd invest in your smile.

Like if it were a new stock on the stock market

and I was in the market to take my nest egg and park it

in the corner crease of your lips,

I am totally sure

that my investment

would absolutely ensure

that I would most certainly procure

a large enough profit

so that I would be able to rest for a while.

I would retire.

Happy, full, breathing and accomplished.

Selah:

Even before they can see,

it has been deemed that babies are conscious.

They listen.

Better than we.

And when they speak,

their native nativity tongue is not nonsense.

It is responsive.

Babies don't come into this world word literate.

Not even a little bit.

Which makes it difficult for us to read the caution signs

between the lines

of every crow's foot

perched over the window seals

of every person

we will soon learn

to love.

Is to lose

and to gain.

A most curious, unusual, propitious type of game.

You only lose when you have.

Having the chance to do again,

I'd do it exactly the same.

Wouldn't change two things.

Just one.

I would have invested it all.

Life is a crap shoot.

You can't win big if you bet too small.

When I was small,

so small in fact that the account of the following subsequent events to me bares more resemblance to folklore than non-fiction;

you would caress my waist

kiss my face

and then carry me past the kitchen

into the living room

and support me for hours on your chest

as I gazed out of the window

and into the livings room.

Out of your giving womb

stemmed forth a flowery forest of life

so vibrant that it might just rival the Amazonias.

Apollonia.

You left.

Earth quakes.

Everything changed.

You would not complain.

I won't complain.

Every time was a present.

Is a present.

I take

shake

open

unwrap

play

embrace

wrap back up

and then stash away.

Eve of Christmas day,

Father calls me to say

that whilst I laid,

God saw fit

to crack ribs

and stole my Eve away.

Guess he could not wait.

How could I blame?

We always did open at least one present that way;

and it was always the best one.

Because it was the giver who chose it.

So as to not ruin the morning,

Saint Nick's gifts come unwrapped.

The most presence is always found in the mourning.

I know there will be mourning.

From the lights of which I cannot hide.

27 minutes past 5

and as of yet, I still have not cried.

Why?

What?

Where I ask is the reason?

Ecclesiastes 3:1

For every matter under Heaven a time

and for everything a season.

Now 'tis the season

to be writing this poem.

At this hour.

In this moment.

As father races to be with daughter.

As sons wish to behold and be held by mothers.

And as the child awakes to shake

and take stock of its gifts.

In the midst of all this...

Today,

God has commissioned the crickets to sing psalms of praise, worship and welcome to the Universe;

And to you.

Beetle Juice

Never audition for a position that you've been wishing to attain.

Because stars,

I mean real stars;

they do not require your permission to burst into existence.

In fact, it is a condition

of subatomic nuclear fission

to transition from simple space dust

when pressed into a dense gravitational position.

Spark the engine and start emitting photonic, supersonic, inoculant flames.

You see,

They just do.

They just come.

They just are.

They just BOOM!

Because stars,

I mean true stars;

they are impatient little crickets in the quiet still of Mississippi night circa 55'.

Charged by the law of hot natured gases

to report to the Universe and its masses

that behind this cloud of tear gases,

crucifix fixed matches,

pillow cases and police chief badges;

that something is alive.

A conscious in the heart of this non-sense.

A circadian rhythm still thrives.

It's a quarter past 5

and the weather is changing.

Do you hear it changing?

Do you see it changing?

Do you feel it changing?

Do you smell it changing?

My grandmother.

She is a weather woman.

She can smell the rain over the hills,

feel the lightning in her steel

and still can see the thunder in a distant location.

Yet and still, even she with her 6th sense for precipitation

has not the slightest inclination

of how these

coronal mass ejections from these

interstellar insurrections are

currently contorting the magnetosphere into visceral dislocation.

So,

if the lack of the facts that my grandmother knows

has no power to slow the neutrinos that go

forward, forth and long beyond towards our home,

like a ball off the bat of The Great Bambino

off into space of off the face of this fiery Helios;

What does that mean for me?

It means,

that I will never apologize

for evaporating the skies

of those who failed to realize

the veracity of the greatness that like steel lies, within my

molten iron, nuclear fired, magnetically spired core.

In the face of your disbelief my sun-rays still stretch forth.

So don't you dare try to limit me whispers this giant red dwarf.

Because my mass is critical.

My vastness, inhospitable.

Meaning maintain your stance in this dance and end up in hospital.

Bulls, crabs, lambs, lion, tigers and bears.

Boeing 747's, the oceans and human hair.

Are all heirs to a throne of accretion and death throes.

Our ship landed in lava but out of the depths rose

We, the children of E=MC squared.

Weigh your heart, not your thoughts.

All the energy is in there.

Because stars,

I mean pure stars;

They are more than just beacons beaming wavelengths into the interstellar bleakness.

They are spherical sticky notes suspended in the mesh of space-time left by God to remind us all

That our time on this terrestrial ball, is small.

So make the most of it all.

Ball.

Get er' done.

Carpe Diem.

Or whatever catchy catch phrase happens to carpe your diem.

Greatness awaits your acquaintance my dear would you like to meet him?

Would you like to meet him?

Would you like to meet him?

Would you like to release him?

Oh, you would?

Ight, cool.

Step 1, is to find your space in this race and run.

Apologize for nothing you are the child of a Sun.

You were made from star stuff, in your blood there is plasma.

So breathe every breath as if you are being choked to death by asthma.

Step 2, is to embrace these number two's.

Examine them for their nuggets.

Don't just flush them down the tube.

Most mistakes are just a case of mistaken identity.

An opportune opportunity to shape and encase our identity.

In a life size cocoon.

Hibernate till the end of June

and in July, be the flyest butterfly this side of the Moon.

Step 3, to me seemed to be the hardest to find.

It is a notion not even confined to the wisest of minds.

Resigned:

Stars give light, but these stars are blind.

Distant stars force us to think, but these stars have no minds.

Stars live out lives dumb, dumbfounding and blind.

To us.

Yet and still,

True stars

I mean real stars

I mean pure star

I mean stars

Still shine.

Kendall Donar was born in Panama City, Fl in 1990. Growing up, his parents heavily encouraged and supported him in all of his artistic endeavors; including prose and poetry. Now 25, this work represents a monumental milestone not only for Kendall, but for those whose loving and supportive shoulders he continues to stand on to this day. He says that though he does thoroughly enjoy writing and performing his works, more than anything he loves to spend quality time and break bread in the company of his friends, family and loved ones in Pensacola, FL; where he presently resides.

"Positive living alters nearly everything."

- **Kendall Donar A.K.A. EFAYEME**

Follow EFAYEME @ Soundcloud.com/efayeme

www.ingramcontent.com/pod-product-compliance
Lightning Source LLC
Chambersburg PA
CBHW060157070426

42447CB00033B/2185

9 780692 661857